MY JOURNEY FROM BAD TO EXCELLENT CREDIT

MY JOURNEY FROM BAD TO EXCELLENT CREDIT

Al Jones

Light Eyes Media™

© 2017 Al Jones
All rights reserved.

ISBN-13: 9780977460151
ISBN-10: 0977460150
Library of Congress Control Number: 2017916154
Light Eyes Media, Phoenix, AZ

This book is dedicated to my parents.

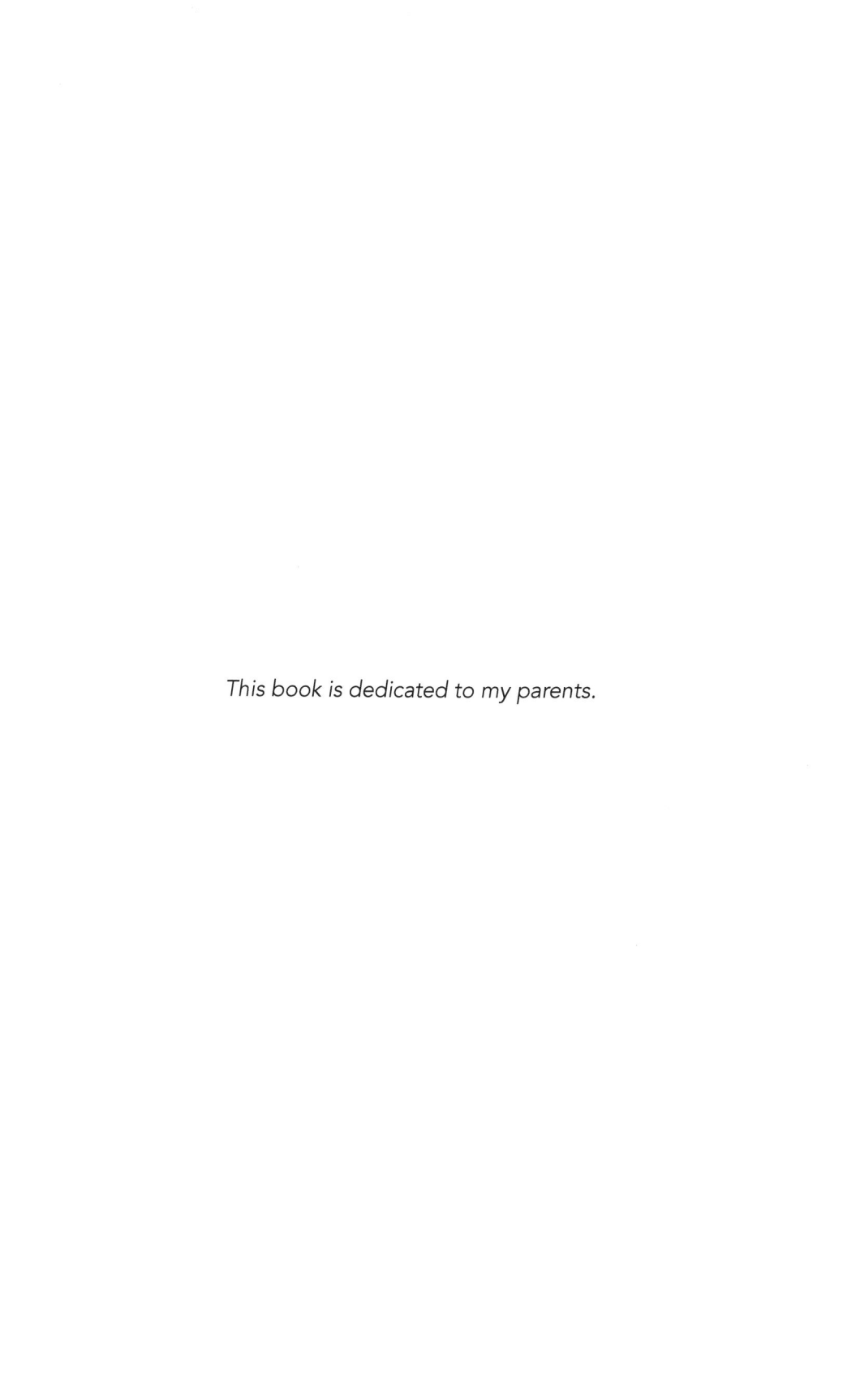

Contents

Introduction ix

1. The Importance of Routines and High Expectations 1
2. Turn your Melted Chocolate Candy into Ice Cream Syrup 5
3. The Importance of Time Management 9
4. The Perils of High Risk Activities 12
5. Decision-making and Emotions 15
6. Repeating Patterns 20
7. Commit to Making a Change for the Better 34
8. Try to Help Others 38
9. Never Quit in Life and Love 41

About the Author 49

Introduction

Our stories may be different, but our desire for quality financial and emotional health is the same. We all have different stories of hardship. No story is more important than the other. My hope is that my story can be a motivating light for you as you travel your own path to financial health. It can assist you in avoiding as many unpleasant experiences as possible, while providing a clear path toward your financial freedom. You now have a friend who understands.

By reading my life story, you will learn the lessons that I had to learn through hard experience. My goal is to provide concrete examples so you can understand key principles about financial decision-making and credit repair.

SUMMARY OF THE LIFE STORY OF AL JONES

Al Jones (born in 1966) is a native of Phoenix, Arizona. Al's childhood consisted of disciplined routines which were the foundation for his later attempts at repairing his credit and changing his life.

As an introvert and mild-mannered adolescent, he was thrust into a more responsible role in the family hierarchy when his parents divorced. In addition to the added responsibilities of general home maintenance, he often answered phone calls from collection agencies for his mother which were demanding payment for past due balances.

My Journey from Bad to Excellent Credit

In high school, he encountered his first opportunity to learn about the positive power of credit, exercised with on the basis of trust and integrity. Enrolled in the United States Army Reserve Officer Training program, Jones participated in a candy bar selling fundraiser and he broke sales records for the program and received multiple accolades for his sales performance.

After graduating from high school, Jones enrolled in in a military junior college with a demanding mental and physical curriculum. His disciplined approach guided him through that phase in his life and enabled him to successfully graduate from the junior college, receive a commission as an Army officer and continue his education.

However, his educational debt load continued to rise. His inability to secure scholarships required he secure additional student loans and credit cards to help finance his education. His mismanagement of time and money as well as the cultural shock from being enrolled in a highly disciplined educational environment to a less structured one, led him to waste a semester's tuition in failed and nearly failed courses. He eventually reduced his procrastination behaviors and regained his focus and graduated with a bachelors degree with honors, but his educational debt was quite significant.

After graduating, Jones was awarded an Army active duty assignment in Korea, an achievement he at first welcomed, but soon he was caught in a cycle of loneliness and gambling. He continued to make bad financial decisions by postponing payment on his student loans, and spending his money on gambling, his mother's debts, and gifts for family and friends.

Jones continued this pattern of bad financial decision-making when he returned to the United States. After receiving an honorable discharge from the military, Jones became unemployed with a medical disability which

Introduction

was rated below eligibility for compensation. He had also accumulated large amounts of credit card and automotive debt as well as his original educational debt that no longer eligible for deferral.

By this time in his life, Jones had established a vicious cycle of bad decision-making: emotions like fear, anxiety and loneliness fuel his hasty and poor financial and life decisions, which result in more anxiety and fear. This cycle explains his first marriage and its failure.

Even when his advanced degree was complete and he found full-time employment at a factory, Jones still felt unappreciated, resentful and fearful. These feelings left him vulnerable to taking out more educational loans to enroll in a doctoral program that he abandoned after one semester. It also left him vulnerable to starting a new relationship with a woman, which followed the same pattern as his first marriage: unemployment, more debt, marriage, stress and anxiety. In addition, the financial burden was becoming inescapable with a mortgage, home repairs and a consolidation loan.

Meanwhile, his sickly mother died. He was one of the beneficiaries named in her insurance policy, so Jones was able to use some of his mother's insurance settlement to pay down some of his existing debt. Shortly after, Jones divorced his second wife, but soon discovered that he had been a victim of identity theft.

Jones grew more frustrated with his life and finally decided that he did not want to repeat the same cycle of behavior and bad decisions. After a long, frustrating process, Jones finally cleared his credit report from the identity theft issues. He also secured a second job as a cab driver. He immersed himself in reading credit repair literature and began to track his own progress. Slowly but surely, Jones was on track to pay down all his debt and began to experience financial freedom.

My Journey from Bad to Excellent Credit

When Jones finally met another woman, he was no longer trapped in the cycle of bad emotions and bad decision. Feeling financially and emotionally secure, he was able to make good decisions about getting into another relationship and becoming financially intertwined with someone. Jones experienced several very happy years with his third wife before she died unexpectedly.

Currently, Jones is securely and happily employed, and is pursuing his goal of supporting people as they travel the path to financial freedom and credit repair.

1

The Importance of Routines and High Expectations

I was born, Alton James Jones, on December 29, 1966, in Phoenix, Arizona, to Jimmie Jones, Jr., a warehouse manager from Arizona and Mildred Jean Jones, a communications equipment assembler from West Virginia.

My parents instilled a daily routine in our home. They also raised us with the notion that children were to be seen and not heard, which most often meant that one did not speak until spoken to.

Weekdays, after waking up we cleaned our rooms, bathed, groomed, ate breakfast, walked to school, returned home, completed homework and chores, ate dinner, briefly watched television, and returned to bed for the night.

Weekends were as demanding.

Our Saturday schedule included scrubbing scuff-marks from walls and baseboards, washing bedroom windows (including sills, screens and glass) and the disposal of pet waste from our lawn. After our chores were completed and inspected we ate breakfast which often included homemade pancakes, coffee, and orange juice.

My Journey from Bad to Excellent Credit

When breakfast was complete, we were given a brief period of rest and watch television, and then we departed to some sort of church activity. Later that evening, we returned home, ate dinner and returned to bed for the night.

Our Sunday schedule included light chores, breakfast, grooming with formal clothing and waiting silently in the formal living room until departing for morning church service. The family vehicle was freshly washed and detailed.

In the car, children sat in the rear seat and quietly rode to church services. Attending services did not mean sitting idle in a pew as a spectator. It involved active participation. In Sunday school, we were expected to interact with the teacher during question and answer period and we took turns reading passages from the weekly workbook aloud.

Before morning church services after Sunday school, we reported to our designated places in either the choir or as an usher. After the church service we returned home, ate dinner, and returned to bed for the night. The weekday cycle returned the following morning.

Elementary school teachers would often comment on my quarterly report cards that I seemed distracted as if I were daydreaming during class. I was.

I grew to be the mild-mannered boy who was often found observing his surroundings, and cautious with his words and actions. It was during those moments of silence that I focused on identifying how I could be the ideal son, please my father and mother, and act as a positive role model to my younger brother and peers – many of those peers who seemed to lack constructive direction and guidance. I hoped my peers would observe my actions and use them as a tool to help them make decisions in their own lives.

My mother and father divorced during my adolescent years. My mind was overwhelmed with mixed emotions – anxiety was the most memorable of

The Importance of Routines and High Expectations

them all. I was afraid that I would fail in my new role as the responsible male of the home.

My mother began working multiple jobs and my sister attended school and worked a part-time job. My younger brother and I shared time together after school at home until Mother returned later that evening from her daily work schedule.

During the evenings when mother was away from home, she would receive multiple calls from collection agencies. Agency representatives would repeatedly call our home during evening hours. Frustrated with the repeated calls, I decided to answer each call, take brief notes of the conversation, and relay it to Mother upon her return.

Conversations with collection agency representatives often included strict and threatening language. My early impression was that these were mean people wanting to scare me and do harm to my mother. As my confidence grew, our conversations became direct with a calm tone. Their confidence grew that the message to her was received and the frequency of call attempts to collect lessened.

Al Jones
2nd Grade

The nightmare continued for years. I wished it would stop.

TIME FOR REFLECTION
Routines and organization vs. unstructured time and chaos

Our childhood has an enormous power to influence our lives. Take a minute to think about your own childhood home and family. Did you have routines, chores and structured expectations? Or did life feel more unstructured, spontaneous and chaotic? Or was it a combination of both?

Describe it here:

What 3 habits or routines from your childhood do you incorporate into your adult life?

What lesson can you find from your childhood that might help you today in your journey to financial freedom? (This lesson can be either positive or negative, i.e. I need to do x, or I shouldn't do y.)

2

Turn your Melted Chocolate Candy into Ice Cream Syrup

The first opportunity to learn about credit and the power of trust from peers outside of my family was in high school.

Mother encouraged enrollment into the United States Army Reserve Officer Training Corps unit. She believed that I would appreciate the disciplined approach to the curriculum. I enrolled in my junior year and quickly realized I had found new opportunities for self-discovery and the observation of human behavior.

I was noticeably taller than many of my unit members and wore an afro. This made my physical appearance awkward when unit members wore similar uniforms and assembled together. Each week, unit members were required to wear a green military uniform. It included polished black leather shoes, black socks, dress slacks and shirt, white t-shirt, black belt, and cap. The uniform was decorated with various badges. I was meticulous in my appearance while wearing it. It was a symbol of pride to me.

Instructors did not assign leadership roles to me, despite the rapid growth in rank. The rationale given was that because I was taller than others, I would serve the unit best if positioned away from them and held its identification flag. This did not alter my desire to succeed in unit activities.

My Journey from Bad to Excellent Credit

Like many educational programs, the unit experienced budget short falls. A fundraising campaign was launched to sell chocolate candy bars. Each unit member was requested to reduce the budget shortfall by selling at least one box of bars. Each box contained multiple bars, all the same flavor and sold for $0.50. I accepted the challenge.

On Wednesdays, I noticed a rapidly growing trend of classmates approaching and wanting to buy candy bars from me. My supply only contained one flavor, so I quickly requested a randomly sorted mix of bar flavors in each box I carried. Soon classmates began to associate the tall guy who wore a groomed uniform with a needed item – sugar. My candy bar sales skyrocketed regardless of whether I wore the uniform that day.

Students who did not have enough funds to pay the full price of a candy bar were extended credit. The amount paid and remaining balance were annotated in the interior of the box. A box was carried throughout each school day and sales did not disrupt classroom flow. Buyers were told that they were trusted to repay balances. In return, many buyers repaid balances within 48 weekday hours.

Buyers often gave tips in appreciation of my flexible payment options. During the fundraising campaign I led in product sales, received multiple awards, gained self-confidence, established trust with peers and generated additional funds gained from tips to contribute to purchasing groceries for my family.

My classmates trusted that I would have an ongoing supply of candy to meet their daily needs. I trusted that they would pay full price for the product sold. My instructor trusted that the boxes of candy issued to me would be sold and that I would return proceed to them in a timely manner.

Turn your Melted Chocolate Candy into Ice Cream Syrup

This event presented the opportunity to make a positive change in my life. It created my desire to make new friends, fall in love, trust someone and believe that people would do what they say.

Credit and trust are mutual.

Al Jones
9th Grade

TIME FOR REFLECTION
Finding opportunity in your everyday life

Think about a time in your life when you "made lemonade out of lemons." How did you turn a hard situation into a great opportunity?

List 3 possible situations in your life right now where you can try to find a new opportunity to improve your finances, self-confidence or relationships.

3

The Importance of Time Management

Enrolling in college out-of-state provided the opportunity to learn new survival skills. The comforts of familiarity were gone.

My mother and I traveled to Roswell, New Mexico, where I was to be enrolled at New Mexico Military Institute, a military junior college. She and I were given a brief tour of the campus by a student leader. The tour concluded with a polite farewell to her. She then slowly walked away while exchanging smiles with the student leader and taking darting glances towards me. The feeling of panic immediately set in when she turned a corner and was no longer visible.

Then it happened!

The attitude of my student leader tour guide immediately changed from mild mannered and personable to loud and demanding. The daily screams and demands placed upon me continued. For me, the emotional feeling was like the experiences of answering the incoming calls from collection agency representatives for my mother. In both instances, I was listening to someone scream at me while demanding results. I felt like I had no control.

However, I did have control. My challenge was discovering its limits.

My Journey from Bad to Excellent Credit

The regimental commander, the most senior student leader, offered us a very memorable lesson. He presented the importance of time management in the daily life of fellow students. When time is effectively managed, it gives one power and opportunity to achieve more. I realized that the more leisure time available to me, the more tempting it was to procrastinate on the completion of tasks and goals. When my daily schedule is filled with activities, my ability to stay focused and on task is enhanced. This also requires prioritizing of tasks and building confidence to reject requests that distract your attention.

Al Jones
R.O.T.C. Basic Training

The establishment of a daily scheduled routine gives you a feeling of control. This feeling will assist you in rejecting elements that distract you from achieving your goal.

The Importance of Time Management

TIME FOR REFLECTION
Time Management

Here are a few activities I incorporate into my daily routine: correspondence, hygiene, laundry, meals, rest.

What activities are in your daily routine?

What activities do you want to put into your daily routine that aren't already there?

How would your life change by putting these activities into a fixed daily schedule?

4

The Perils of High Risk Activities

It was common during college orientation for credit card companies to display booths on campus. They would offer gifts of gratitude for applying for a new credit card.

Because of my low grades during high school, I had limited options for paying for college. As a result, student loans were my primary source of tuition funding, along with credit cards and a small stipend from the military.

After years of college enrollment and military service in the United States and Korea, I accumulated a sizeable amount of financial debt. Choices such as irresponsible credit card spending, paying only the minimum monthly card balances, and deferring student loan payments made the problem worse.

When I was assigned to a remote unit in South Korea, I was very lonely. Soon, I found myself going to local clubs to gamble. Soft music, video poker and slot machines, friendly female attendants and a few glasses of soft drinks were the recipe for my self-destruction. Playing the machines appeared to be a harmless alternative to drinking.

I always planned to cash my payroll check, take a few dollars to the club, chat with many of the attractive female attendants, play a few rounds on

The Perils of High Risk Activities

the machines and leave. However, the convenience of ATMs positioned in the clubs made it more convenient to use your credit card to withdraw a cash advance or debt card to withdraw from your checking or savings account.

I did not drink nor smoke, but the smell of alcohol and cigarette smoke within the clubs did not deter me from visiting. When the clubs would close for business hours, I would often stand outside and look through the windows to watch the employees inside. I felt sadness each night as I watched chain-smoking employees frantically playing multiple machines. They played as if attempting to trigger wins and collect the money I wasted.

Al Jones
Han River, Seoul, Korea

TIME FOR REFLECTION
High Risk Activities

Discuss any habitual high-risk activity in your life that causes (or has caused) the greatest amount of financial loss. Explain why you chose to participate and the feelings you encountered.

5

Decision-making and Emotions

I lived within the military installation. I frequently sent money to my mother to help her with her expenses including travel, car accessories, food and paying the minimum credit card balances.

Then it happened.

I had not prepared emotionally or financially for what would happen. I was at the rifle range with my unit, target practicing with my rifle. It was one of the best target practicing experiences I had in years. I qualified as an expert rifleman.

My immediate supervisor and her immediate supervisor waited until I finished with target practice. I was directed to walk towards them. Once I greeted them, I was then directed to evaluate my rifle to ensure there were no bullets remaining in neither the barrel nor magazine.

Once my rifle was safe, they announced that my term of service would expire in 30 days. I quickly pleaded for an additional 30 days which were eventually granted to me. I felt ashamed standing in front of my co-workers, while being told by management my service was no longer needed.

I was granted an honorable discharge from the United States Army. I was proud that I had served, yet I was an unemployed veteran, with a disability rating level too low to qualify for compensation. I had limited cash and lots of bills to pay.

Months prior to receiving notification of my discharge, I met a woman. She was a fellow officer who was rapidly advancing in promotional status in her field of medicine.

We were dating and upon discharge notification, I asked if I could move into her apartment. It was my hope that I could stay with her for a few months while seeking employment in the state. Then, once employed, we could depart as friends.

Month after month, day after day, my anxiety grew as I opened the mail to read employment rejections and past due bill notifications. I then thought I should act and protect my ego. I would save myself from the anguish of returning home to my immediate family as a perceived failure. I proposed marriage to her. She accepted.

My weekly job search routine included a grueling 75-mile one-way commute to the State of Texas' Employment Commission office, which offered job service counseling. Each Thursday for nearly seven months, I would submit a written job search claim form, visit a job service counselor, and seek a referral to an employment opportunity.

My mood was optimistic during each appointment. I set each appointment with the same counselor at the same time and day of the week. I hoped that the counselor would recognize my persistence and notify a hiring employer about this trait during the referral process.

There I was, with just two weeks remaining before my extended unemployment compensation would end. I sat in the chair next to my counselor and greeting him with a smile. In a humorous manner, I then mentioned

Decision-making and Emotions

that due to the frequency of my visits, someone should place me on the State's payroll. I was unaware of who was observing my behavior and actively listening nearby.

My counselor smiled and chuckled. He looked at me and quickly positioned toward the man standing behind me. It was the office manager. Suddenly, I felt a hand on my shoulder and a man's voice asking if I would like to work for him and the State of Texas. I nearly cried.

During this period, my fiancée and I wed and moved into a new home. My net pay after paying my personal debt was approximately $100 per month. My wife was the primary wage earner of the family. I maintained the daily upkeep of the home. Feelings of sadness and anxiety soon followed.

She suggested I enroll in a nearby university to further my education with a graduate degree in management science with an emphasis in the management of healthcare facilities. Evening courses were available. I welcomed her advice, applied for another student loan and enrolled, further increasing my financial debt.

It was only a matter of time before the increased time away from each other brought further uncertainty to the relationship. She was rapidly advancing in her profession as a health care provider. I felt that I was a financial liability rather than an asset to the relationship.

One night during a discussion, I decided to separate from my wife. I had a few dollars in my checking account, mounting debt and a few dollars of available credit on credit cards. I returned the following day in my car to collect work clothes and small personal items. A former co-worker lived nearby and invited me to stay at his home until I felt more confident about leaving. I stayed for less than a week. It was long enough to collect my next paycheck, secure additional employment and a new place to live – a studio apartment.

My Journey from Bad to Excellent Credit

To my horror, I discovered that the unit was German roach infested. I exterminated. I slept in my car at night, while storing clothing in the unit. I searched each day to find an advertisement for a used couch in the local newspaper. When the couch was delivered, I discovered that it was not wide enough to stretch my legs fully during sleep. I rotated sleeping on the couch or floor to ease the discomfort.

My daily diet consisted of lemon water, and a week of homemade chili, spaghetti, or a whole roasted chicken. I no longer had the daily 75-mile weekday commute to work. However, I had to drive the same round-trip commute twice a week to continue evening school courses. The degree program lasted nearly three years. I completed the graduate program with honors.

In the process, my marriage failed. It lasted less than a year.

Decision-making and Emotions

TIME FOR REFLECTION
Decision-making and Emotion

When faced with situations that made me feel anxious, insecure and fearful, I began to make decisions, particularly about relationships, that only contributed to my financial problems.

What kinds of decisions do you make when you are feeling anxious, insecure or fearful? Do you avoid making decisions at all or do you rush into things without thinking through all the consequences?

Looking back on your past bad decisions, what advice would you give to yourself now?

6

Repeating Patterns

After years of living in the studio apartment and the completion of the graduate school program, my confidence grew. A local factory held a job fair. I had applied for a job at the factory in the past, but was not hired. In the previous interview, a manager asked me where I saw myself in five years. My deadpan response to him was---his job.

It was obvious, a new approach was needed.

Later, another job fair at the factory was announced. I was more determined not to fail in the interview process. Advanced research revealed that the factory actively recruited members of a national trade organization. I quickly joined the organization, added it to my resume and submitted it to the factory for employment consideration. Days later, I was invited to the job fair for employment consideration.

During the group interview process, members of the team repeatedly commented on their pleasure that I was an active member of the trade organization—it was clear that they did not know that I had joined days prior to the interview. I was invited and returned for a second interview a few days later. A job offer was made to me. I accepted.

The new salary allowed me to increase the amount paid towards my existing credit card and auto loan debt. However, the lingering student loan debt remained. I thought I needed to further delay payment of my student loan debt. If I did, I could then move to a one-bedroom apartment, purchase a real bed and improve my lifestyle. Shortly, I moved within the same apartment complex to a one-bedroom unit. I had to somehow delay my pending educational debt.

I received an advertisement for a distance learning educational institution in the mail with congratulations on the recent completion of my graduate degree program. It further referenced potential employment opportunities for those who earned post-graduate degree.

This sounded like a great solution--I could apply for more student loans to finance my education, delay existing student loan debt and complete the doctoral program. I would then earn enough salary to pay off all pending debt. In addition, earning a doctorate in business administration and being called Doctor Jones triggered the emotion of ego in me. When the program was complete, employers would fight to hire me.

But you know what happened? Within a year after receiving the loan and enrolling into the program, the dream died. I suddenly lost interest in obtaining a doctoral degree and disenrolled in the program. However—the debt remained.

Then it happened, again.

I had not prepared emotionally or financially for what would happen. Factory employees were notified that personnel cuts were pending. I had been employed at the factory a year and had been granted a significant promotion in rank within my field. Shortly, others within my department were tapped on the shoulder by a staff member of the personnel department. Fired employees were handed a cardboard box to pack personal items and walked to an exit nearby. A security offer collected badges and the personnel staff member distributed literature about the company's outplacement process. As you exited, the door closed from behind.

It was like a repeating nightmare.

By this time, I was dating again, so I asked the new woman I was dating if I could move into her apartment. Once again, it was my hope that I could stay with her for a few months while seeking employment in the state. Month after month, day after day, anxiety grew as I opened mail to read employment rejection and past due bill notifications.

Reluctantly, I informed my mother that my employment situation was not as bright as I had led her to believe. She was shocked as much as I was disappointed in myself. She offered a room in her home until I was more confident.

I left Texas and the woman I had dated while there. We continued a long-distance relationship. The plan was for her to relocate and move into a home with me, once I could secure stable employment in Arizona.

My weekly job search routine included weekly meetings at a job service center associated with State of Arizona's Department of Economic Security. Each week for nearly seven months, I would submit a written job search claim form, visit a job service counselor, and seek a referral to an employment opportunity.

I approached this with same attitude—optimistic and determined, hoping that my persistence would be rewarded. Yet here I was again, with just two weeks remaining before my extended unemployment compensation would end. Finally, I received a call to schedule a job interview.

I completed the job interview and was offered employment. My family was happy with the positive news. My hope was that I would now be

Repeating Patterns

able to begin repaying my debt and life would change for the better. The woman to whom I was engaged was also happy and we prepared for her relocation.

I soon moved out of my mother's home and found an apartment for my fiancée and me. She quit her job at the same factory from where I had been recently fired and but she did not secure employment in Arizona before she left. When she arrived, I was optimistic in finding new and steady employment for her. My optimism was short lived as her weeks and months of unemployment continued. We were both feeling sadness and anxiety about the situation. So, we eloped.

We tried starting multiple business ventures together which generated limited income. We could pay some old debt, but quickly accumulated new and combined debt.

Al Jones' Starter Home
6510 W. Heatherbrea Dr.
Phoenix, AZ 85033

My Journey from Bad to Excellent Credit

Years later, we located a small starter home and moved out of the apartment we had been renting. We were advised that I should be the sole name on the mortgage, due to the condition of her credit profile. The loan was approved and we were anxious to move into our new place. It was a vintage home, built in 1960s. It had a big back yard in a quiet neighborhood. It was the first home I owned and it was located a few streets away from the home I used to live in as a child.

We expected to encounter a few minor problems after a few years of purchase, but we did not anticipate encountering a major problem within months. We paid for a home inspection prior to our purchase in order to identify potential problems. However, months after the purchase, the HVAC was broken. We lived in a vintage home and the new equipment required the installation of new duct-work. We did not have cash readily available, so I contacted a local subprime lender to assist.

I applied and qualified for multiple debt consolidation loans. The second mortgage was used to pay for the new HVAC repair and installation. My personal debt level further increased.

Eventually, lending agencies began calling my office demanding payment. Imagine being in a supervisory role in an open work environment with coworkers sharing cubicles nearby. You are trying desperately to maintain composure while answering incoming calls from lending institutions. You hope that the repeated incoming collection calls do not cause disciplinary action and lead to your job loss.

My mother, who was battling cancer as well as mounting debt from financial mismanagement, noticed a change in my appearance. She knew that one of the early signs that I was experiencing extreme difficulty is my weight dropping. She lived a few minutes away and would randomly call, claiming she was experiencing problems with her personal computer. I would leave home during evening hours to remedy her problem, only to

Repeating Patterns

discover no repair was needed. She had just wanted to chat while sharing a pot of coffee.

She was a religious woman and died on Good Friday of the year 2000. I received her insurance beneficiary payment and it helped me pay off some of the financial debt I accumulated over my lifetime. It was what I desperately needed—but what a cost I had to pay.

My feelings of anger and resentment continued to build after years of my wife not securing full-time employment. It was my opinion that we were both living in a toxic home environment and so I requested a divorce. In turn, she visited the local court, and filed instead. We agreed that both would stay in the home until sold. It had negative equity.

Soon a buyer expressed interest in purchasing the property. He and I agreed on a price. The property was sold for the balance due on the primary mortgage. Later, he agreed to pay the remaining balance of the second mortgage to finalize the property purchase transaction. In exchange for paying the second mortgage and freeing me from that mortgage debt obligation, I would sign a promissory note to him. Monthly payment installments would be paid directly to him. He set the payment terms.

My second wife and I moved out of the property. She received a financial settlement, home furnishings and the newer of the two vehicles. We each moved to separate apartments within the city. She subsequently moved back to Texas.

Soon after she left, I became the victim of identity theft. I'm not accusing her of theft. However, something happened between the time we moved out of the property and her return to Texas. I began to receive calls from telecommunications companies stating that accounts in the state of Texas had been established using my name. The accounts for each were at least 90 days past due, required assistance of a collection agency and must be paid immediately.

My Journey from Bad to Excellent Credit

I had to find an additional source of income and I refused to file bankruptcy because I thought it would mean I would be considered a failure. My life consisted of years of financial mismanagement from poor lifestyle choices. How could I face myself each day knowing I did not atone for my past mistakes?

I applied for and completed the required driver training to become a cab driver. I started work on a 12-hour shift Friday night after an eight-hour weekday job. The weekday job would end, I would go home to change clothing and then commute to the cab depot. I would return home Saturday morning to rest. Saturday evening, I would return to the cab depot to begin another 12-hour shift, and then return Sunday morning to rest.

Hours sitting in the cab alone waiting for a customer provided the venue to gain clarity in life. This led to the idea of making a more diligent effort to make improvements, and write about the experiences I faced. Were there occurrences as a driver where my life was in danger? Yes! It didn't matter; I had bills to pay.

I was still battling with the drama involved with being a victim of identity theft. I had read other stories about identity theft, but I didn't think that it could happen to me. I was wrong.

The advice given to me was to contact the local police office in the city associated with the account established with the fraudulent identification. An officer assigned to identity theft claims received a summary of my problem and assigned a case number to me.

The burden of proof was now my responsibility. I had to prove to each agency that I did not live in the State of Texas at the time the accounts were established. If I could not, I was advised that I would be responsible for the past due balances owed on each account and my credit reports would continue to reflect my alleged negative payment history. Agencies

Repeating Patterns

demanded a copy of my tenant rental agreement as well as other financial documents mailed to my true address during the period in question.

However, during this period, I had rented an apartment and did not keep a copy of the annual rental agreement. The property was sold, so my rental period shortened and I was required to vacate.

I purchased a credit report and score separately from each of the three main credit bureaus. Today, one can order their personal credit report online with the convenience of an electronic copy for review. I had to wait days for each printed copy to be sent to me by postal mail. Upon receipt, I reviewed each report and documented which account was established with my fraudulent identification.

Camelback Towers Apartments
4750 N. Central Ave.
Phoenix, AZ 85012

I also purchased a permanent security freeze on my personal credit profile from each of the three credit bureaus. This process was designed to prevent lenders and others from accessing your credit profile to generate a new line of credit. When a permanent freeze status is on the existing credit profile, the consumer must contact the bureau used by the desired lender and purchase a temporary thaw. When the thaw period ends, the freeze status returns on the credit profile.

The challenging element was establishing proof of residency.

Years had passed since occupying the apartment unit during the period. Why would the property owner of an apartment building planned for conversion to condominiums archive printed copies of tenant rental payments maintained by the seller? At first I was discouraged--what were the odds of these documents being available to me? Then, I remembered obtaining the contact information of the sales representative of the new property owner prior to vacating my unit. I called her.

She remembered the conversation we had about the development of the property. Since our conversation, she had purchased the converted unit I previously occupied, and she was happy with it. I explained the dilemma I faced with identity theft and the requirement to prove occupancy at the property. It was her opinion that in the property transfer process and remodel, the former apartment tenant rental agreements were packed and stored. She needed time to investigate.

Meanwhile, I continued to receive regularly scheduled calls from collection agencies demanding the status of my effort to supply proof of residency. Weeks later, I was informed by the sales agent of the new property owner that she had located a few boxes which might include the agreement I needed. A few days later, she informed me that she had found a copy of my agreement and faxed a copy of it to me. It was exactly what I needed—and it was an emotional moment that I would never forget.

I printed and forwarded a copy of the rental agreement and other related documents to the collectors. Weeks later, I received letters from each of them confirming that I was no longer responsible for the debt and that any negative history relating to it would be removed from my personal credit profile. I kept checking my credit reports and soon, the negative credit history associated with the stolen identity was removed from my credit reports.

I have yet to contact that city's police department to inquire about the status of the case. It was my opinion at the time that little would be done

Repeating Patterns

to prosecute these criminals. A case number would be issued for tracking and records of the crime would be stored away in a banker's box as an open case. It was the responsibility of the victim to further remedy problem with lenders. I was treated like I was guilty until proven innocent.

TIME FOR REFLECTION
Repeating Patterns

Unemployment, a second marriage and divorce, more consumer and educational debt—I had been through these experiences already. But why did I repeat them?

Anxiety. This is a POWERFUL emotion. Identify what makes you anxious and be open to taking steps toward its control.

Do these events trigger your anxiety? If so, explain why.

1. Birthdays
2. Christmas
3. Discussion of death
4. Discussion of divorce
5. Donation requests
6. Door knocking
7. Grocery shopping
8. Receiving mail
9. Personal illness
10. Telephone ringing

Repeating Patterns

11. Unemployment

12. Vehicle repair

Are there more you can think of? List and discuss below.

TAKING CONTROL
If any of these events trigger anxiety, you are NOT alone. The events listed were specifically chosen because they all triggered anxiety in me. Look at my response to each event and how I controlled my anxiety:

Birthdays
- My love and time spent with you is more valuable than any material item.

Christmas
- Celebrate how you want.
- Do not feel guilty for declining a party invitation or rejecting offers of food.

Discussion of death
- Openly discuss your wishes upon death with family and friends.
- Identify a trusted family member or friend to be the executor of your estate to help ensure your wishes are met upon death.
- Prepare a will and establish a medical power of attorney. Ensure both documents are notarized and have the correct number of witnesses as required by law.

Discussion of divorce
    If your opinion is that a divorce settlement is necessary, locate a place to organize your thoughts about how to:

My Journey from Bad to Excellent Credit

- Identify your wants and needs.
- Identify what you think your spouse may want and need.
- Identify what you think your spouse will think about your wants and needs, as well as their own.
- Meet with your spouse in a safe and neutral environment to discuss and compare wants and needs.
- Negotiate a settlement.

Donation requests
- Do not feel ashamed if you decline.

Door knocking
- Create a sign and attach it to the main door used to enter your home. The sign should state that solicitors should not disturb you.

Grocery shopping
- Eat a snack before you leave to shop. It may help you resist the temptation to purchase additional food items on impulse.
- Create a detailed shopping list before you enter the store to stay focused.

Receiving mail
- Expect direct mail advertising to be placed in your mailbox on Wednesdays.
- Visit www.OptOutPrescreen.com to manage the volume of advertising you receive.

Personal illness
- Make an appointment with a health care provider to schedule an annual exam.
- Request assistance in creating a preventive maintenance routine.

Repeating Patterns

Telephone ringing
- Turn on voicemail.
- Reduce the number of rings on your phone before it advances to voicemail.
- Set ringer to mute and display a visible notification of a missed call.
- Google Voice service can record and dictate incoming messages.

Unemployment
- Familiarize yourself with changing trends of your employment industry.
- Seek opportunities to advance existing job skills.
- Search the Dictionary of Occupational Titles and identify transferrable job titles in other sectors.

Vehicle repair
- Get a recommended maintenance schedule for the make and model of your vehicle.
- Identify what repairs you are comfortable performing and those you are not.
- Contact friends, family and seek a referral to someone willing to barter auto repair services for a special skill you have.
- Familiarize yourself with and use mass transit services available in your area.
- Nap, meditate, and reduce stress during your mass transit commute.

How do you manage events that trigger anxiety?

7

Commit to Making a Change for the Better

I continued to work my full-time weekday job and drive the cab at night on weekends to attempt to lower my personal debt. I was determined not to file bankruptcy regardless of how frugal my life had to be. I wanted to exemplify to others the consequences of personal finance mismanagement and the moral choices I made for redemption. It was time to commit to making a change in my life and helping others. I could give them clear guidelines to dramatically enhance their individual credit performance.

I was familiar with an environment where it was common to have repeated calls for collection of past due balances. I found opportunities to delay payment of a loan in order to pay a different loan. However, I had now become frustrated with the direction my life had been going. I did not want to return to how it was before, but was confused with what the future would be like for me.

So, I continued to work multiple jobs with long hours, utilize public transit, and eat less. I admit that my diet was poor. I slept less than my preferred daily limit and dark circles around my eyes were plainly obvious. To my delight, coffee was a daily staple and still is to this day.

However, I was making progress.

For instance, I learned how to establish a settlement agreement with the collection agency to resolve a delinquent balance. The borrower offers to

Commit to Making a Change for the Better

make a payment towards the delinquent balance with a condition. When the borrower pays the agreed balance, the agency responds in writing confirming receipt of payment and commits to the deletion of negative credit history from the personal credit profile. This is an alternative for the agencies to quickly collect vs extending resources to try to collect a full balance over a lengthier period.

I created a bill payment process with the use of a standard calendar which incorporates a bi-weekly pay day cycle. Use the first paycheck of the month and pay, that day, the bills due between that date of payment and the day prior to your second paycheck. Days are referenced with the letter, A.

Use the second paycheck of the month and pay, *that day*, the bills due between that date of payment and the day prior to the first pay check of the following month. Days are referenced with the letter, B.

SUN	MON	TUE	WED	THU	FRI	SAT
1 B	2 B	3 B	4 B	5 B	6 Pay A	7 A
8 A	9 A	10 A	11 A	12 A	13 A	14 A
15 A	16 A	17 A	18 A	19 A	20 Pay B	21 B
22 B	23 B	24 B	25 B	26 B	27 B	28 B
29 B	30 B	31 B				

My Journey from Bad to Excellent Credit

Continue this bi-weekly bill payment cycle even when there are three pay dates in that month. Billing statements will arrive referencing "$0.00 Due" for that month's cycle.

If the monthly payment amount for that bill (e.g., cell phone) varies, make an advanced payment based on the estimated amount you have paid over approximately three months. Send an additional payment, if you receive a statement referencing any additional funds due which were more than your advanced payment.

Over the life of the loan, you will notice a reduction in the total amount of interest being paid.

Commit to Making a Change for the Better

TIME FOR REFLECTION
Commit to Making a Change for the Better

List 3 financial ideas or tools you want to learn more about.

What is your plan to find the information about these ideas or tools?

What are 3 small things you can do every month to make a difference in your financial routines and decision-making?

8

Try to Help Others

When a past due balance was paid and settled with a lender, I would order a credit report and score separately from each of the three credit bureaus. My credit score based on each of the bureau's algorithms continued to rise. The ordering and receiving a new credit report with a higher score became somewhat of a symbolic event. My thoughts began to drift towards how to make a difference in other people's lives with my own personal journey from credit disaster to credit repair.

So, I began to order, reformat, and sell redacted electronic copies of each of my credit reports. The goal was to illustrate the profile formula of someone with good credit.

I traveled to Washington DC to participate in financial literacy discussions. I have also been interviewed on television and radio new programs about financial literacy. I created a weblog with integrated rich site summary (RSS) technology to generate discussion about personal finance and financial literacy. Helpful content was posted daily. However, it generated limited traction and I shut it down.

The sales of the redacted copy of my personal credit reports were less than my first book. Here I was, willing to share my personal information with the public, attempt help others and received few takers. The next

Try to Help Others

plan was to offer paid seminars on the topic of personal finance. Many doubted its validity and few came to listen.

The idea of using social media and the creation of an interactive webpage appealed to me. I discovered a website where one could create and respond to short videos in a question-and-answer format. If a question was sent to me, I would receive notification of that incoming question with the option to respond with a video. I would upload the file to the site and share the link to it with other social media websites. Sadly, after months of use and building relationships, the website shut down. Requests for copies of video files uploaded to the site went unanswered.

My final push was the creation of public service announcements which provided helpful hints to consumers. The PSAs were 60-seconds in duration. Radio stations could use them to fill time vacancies between programs and advertisements. I spent hours sending query letters to radio stations and agents to gain traction. Most emails remained unanswered.

It was my opinion that all consumers needed to hear what I had to say about financial mismanagement. Maybe I was trying to save those who did not want to be saved. Maybe it was their acceptance of willful ignorance. Reality hits hard.

I withdrew the paperback and electronic books from bookstores for resale. Many paperbacks scheduled for sale were just given away as random gifts. Later, I discovered that those gifted books became items for sale on the websites of eBay and Amazon. This offered little consolation to my feeling of despair.

Then, I met another woman…

My Journey from Bad to Excellent Credit

TIME FOR REFLECTION
Try to Help Others

Whether you believe in the Golden Rule, Karma (what goes around comes around) or leaving the world in a better place than when you entered it—the goal of helping others as you travel the credit repair path is a great one. I don't mean that you should help others by giving them money—you can help them by providing a good financial example, modeling good decision-making practices and providing emotional support and love.

What are the 3 most important non-money gifts you have received from others in your life?

Pick one, and make a plan to "pay it forward." How will you do this?

What is the most important thing you are learning about financial decision-making through this book?

How can you model that for others?

9

Never Quit in Life and Love

During this period in my life, my credit was rated as good. My only outstanding debt was a vehicle loan. Generating a new application for a mortgage was not of interest to me. Neither was marriage.

Al Jones' view from condominium building
Executive Towers Condominiums
207 W. Clarendon Ave
Phoenix, AZ 85013

My Journey from Bad to Excellent Credit

I was living a comfortable life as a confirmed bachelor. I rented a one-bedroom condominium in a high-rise building. The view overlooking the city's skyline was spectacular. It was the bachelor pad of my dreams. I also had a sports car, trendy furniture, steady employment, and a few nice clothes to wear. What more did I need?

Then, she appeared.

She was standing in the condominium's mailroom reading mail. Have you ever approached someone for the first time and instantly knew that something special was going to happen between the two of you? That is what I felt at that very moment.

I entered the mailroom; we smiled, exchanged greetings to one another and acted coy. My heart raced with anticipation as I retrieved my mail, exchanged a farewell with the woman and returned home to my unit. A mental note was made as to what time and day of the week I had met this woman. My hope was that I would be able to see her again.

The same time, same day of the following week arrived and I walked towards the mailroom. The same woman, standing in the mailroom reading her mail, was there again.

Once again I entered the mailroom; we smiled, exchanged greetings to one another and acted coy. My heart raced with anticipation as I retrieved my mail, exchanged a farewell with the woman and walked towards the exit.

The next time we saw each other in the mailroom, she asked my name and whether I had plans that night for dinner. My normal dinner routine was to eat a light salad at home alone, conduct research on the Internet and go to bed. She offered to drive and pay for dinner for the both of us. I accepted her offer.

Never Quit in Life and Love

We became friends. She was financially savvy and aware of the importance in achieving and maintaining good credit. She had retired from multiple employers and had become bored with the slow pace of retirement life. She wanted a new job to keep her occupied. We were both military veterans and shared a dry wit.

She was offered a job out of state and she accepted. She asked that I watch and maintain her unit while still leasing my own. We corresponded daily and grew closer as friends. Months later, she quit the job and decided to return to the state to be with me.

Shortly, she suggested that I end the lease of my existing unit and move into her unit together. You can imagine how my mind began to race. I had been married twice, as had she. Why would I want to give up my bachelor life and move out of the unit I came to adore? Why would I be willing to take the risk? What was happening to me?

Soon, the desire to return to a full-time job no longer appealed to her. I was still employed at my full-time job. She was financially secure with multiple pensions. She relished the brief chats we had on the phone each day while I was away at work. She waited for me on a bench outside the building to return home from work. She became giddier the closer I approached. Each day, I felt as if I was a heroic soldier who had returned home to a victory parade. The nickname she gave to me was "Love Doll Baby."

Frustrated with the repeated plumbing problems experienced in the unit she owned, she decided it would be best to sell it and buy a new unit with me. Trust had been established while watching and maintaining her property. She expressed commitment by quitting her job to return and live with me. Why not?

Her property eventually sold. We purchased a bigger unit together on a higher floor in the building. The deed referenced us as a single man and a single woman. In six months of living together in the new unit, I proposed marriage. She accepted.

As a joint mortgage holder who made timely payments, my credit score quickly increased. The only other debt I held was an auto loan and soon, the full balance of that loan was paid in full. It was paid before the scheduled payoff date, because I had made additional payments towards the principal balance. In fact, she insisted that I do so.

She grew tired of preparing dinner for the two of us and suggested that we begin a ritual of eating out each night instead. It was her opinion that she deserved to have more fun during retirement. She worked most of her life and now was the time to enjoy what she worked hard to achieve. She wanted to share this time in her life with someone special. She had become proud of my persistence in maintaining responsible behavior in personal finance.

She insisted that each nightly meal would be charged to my credit card. In turn, she would pay the balance. Soon each expense, large or small, was charged to my credit card and the balance was paid in full. The use of my credit card for the purchase of household electronics enabled us to leverage the feature of extending the manufacturer's warranty. Reward points were immediately generated from credit card use. We frequently redeemed points for gift items. Lenders began to automatically increase credit limits on my cards. She wanted me to have an excellent credit rating as much as I did. My credit score was skyrocketing!

Then it happened. She died.

We had been married seven years. She passed just four months from our eighth wedding anniversary. However, I still continue her prescribed daily ritual of dining out each night, charging items large or small on my credit card and paying the full balance each month. Periodically, I would let a few dollars on the balance be charged interest.

As of now, I have an 846 out of 850 FICO® Score 8 credit rating.

TIME FOR REFLECTION
Never Quit in Life and Love

For me, the third marriage was the charm—but I wish it had taken me less time to reverse my destructive behaviors. But with time and persistence, I finally achieved all my goals and felt happy and secure.

What has taken you a long time to learn and to finally get right?

How did you keep hope until things started going your way?

What advice would you give yourself to make that positive outcome come more quickly?

Never Quit in Life and Love

Scan this code to view my credit score confirmation page.

If you have made it to this page, congratulations! You have now not only discovered my survival behavior, but how my current credit status was achieved. It may not take you as long nor be as dramatic. If you focus today and commit to making a change to your personal credit profile, in time you will succeed.

About the Author

Al Jones has had his own challenges with credit. Financial mistakes and a case of identity theft tanked his score and led to many other issues. Jones knew something had to change. He started educating himself about credit repair and eventually raised his FICO® Score 8 credit rating to 846/850. He now wants to share his success with you!

Jones is a native son of Phoenix, Arizona. After being honorably discharged from the US Army, he moved back to his hometown and created the Al Jones Corporation. The Al Jones Corporation is a game-development company dedicated to creating user-friendly games for mobile devices, live shows, playing cards, and more.